A Secret History of

Coffee, Coca & Cola

The Second Part OF THE

WORKS

OF

Mr Ricardo Cortés,

BEING

His Books of Plants,

Viz. { The *First* of MARIJUANA.
{ The *Second* of COFFEE, KOLA, and COCA

Now made English *by several Hands.*

With a Necessary INDEX.

Licensed and Entered,

BROOKLYN

Published by Akashic Books • ©2012 Ricardo Cortés

ISBN-13: 978-1-61775-134-9

Library of Congress Control Number: 2012939267

Akashic Books

PO Box 1456 • New York, NY 10009

info@akashicbooks.com • www.akashicbooks.com

for Ma & Pa

It is amusing to now look back at some attacks which were hurled against substances that all the world to-day considers as necessities . . .

How real must be the merit that can withstand such storms of abuse, and spring up, perennially blooming, through such opposition!

W. Golden Mortimer
History of Coca
1901

Table of Contents

You wicked child,
disobedient girl,
Oh, when will I get my way
that you quit that coffee!
　　　　　—*Schlendrian*

Father, don't be so rough.
If I can't have my coffee three times a day,
I will become, to my dismay,
like a dried-up goat steak.
　　　　　—*Liesgen*

Johann Sebastian Bach
Kaffee Kantate
1734

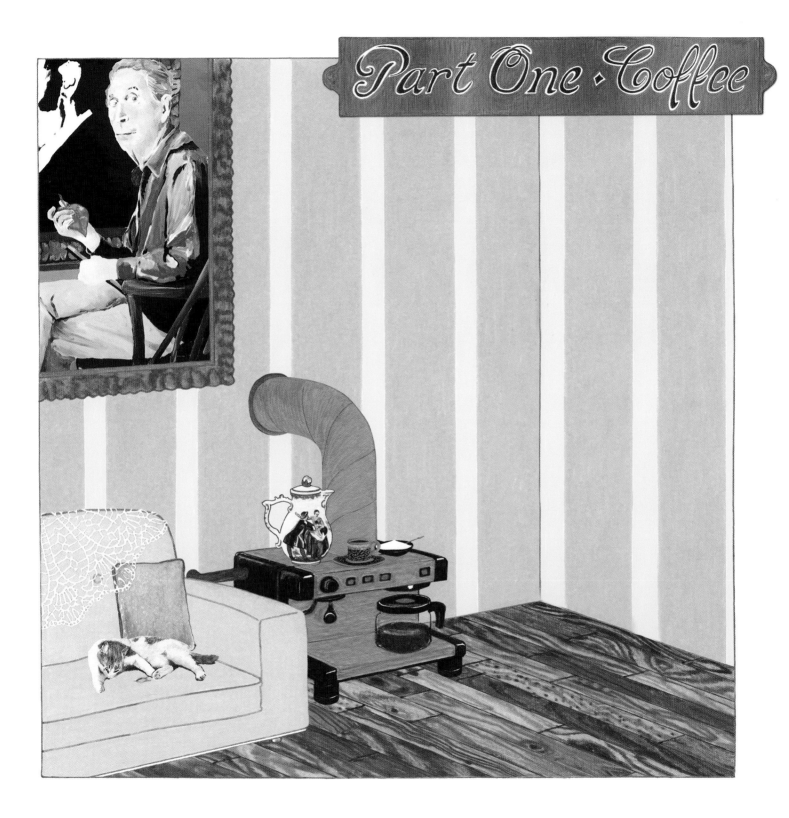

Part One · Coffee

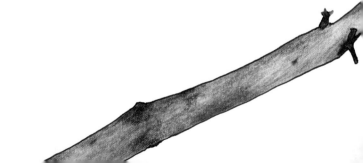

One story about the origin of coffee is that of a goatherd, tending goats on a mountainside in Ethiopia.

The goats, tired and hungry, stopped to chew on some cherries and began to grow very frisky.

The cherry seemed to drive away fatigue. People tried roasting the seeds inside and brewing them to drink. Speculation rose about its healing properties.

From Ethiopia, the cherry traveled to Yemen.

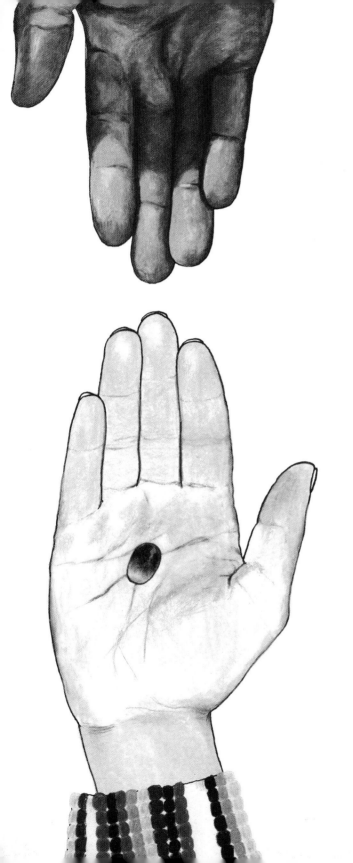

By the sixteenth century, *qahwah* was available throughout the Islamic world. Debate began about the salubrity, morality, and legality of the intoxicating plant.

As interest grew, opponents tried to end its use and punish traffickers. In 1511, the beverage was banned in the Arabian city of Mecca—a short-lived prohibition, but similar bans emerged in Cairo and elsewhere. Dealers were beaten, inventories burned.

According to accounts of the sixteenth-century historian Îbrahim Peçevî, when *kahveh* arrived in Turkey it was met with opposition from sultans who forbade the bean under penalty of death.

By the seventeenth century *coffee* reached Europe, portrayed alternately as a health remedy ("for Head-ach," "Cough of the Lungs," and "very good to prevent Mis-carryings") and as a cause of maladies like melancholia, mind degeneration, and impotence. Coffeehouses were called sites of vice and sedition.

In 1675, King Charles II issued an edict for their suppression.

BY THE KING,
A Proclamation.

WHEREAS, it is most apparent that the multitude C O F F E E Houses set up within this kingdom have produced very evil and dangerous effects; as well for that many tradesmen and others, do herein mispend much of their time, which might and probably would be employed in and about their Lawful Calling and Affairs; but also, for that in such houses divers false, malitious and scandalous reports are devised and spread to the Defamation of his Majestie's Government, and to the Disturbance of the Peace and Quiet of the Realm; his Majesty hath thought fit and necessary, that the said Houses be, for the future, Put down, and suppressed.

December 23. 1675

PETITION
AGINST
A BEAN

Caution & Strike Fear in your children, prone to the fancy Enfeebling whims lurking within a Newfangled, Abominable, Dangerous & Heathenish Liquor

HELP keep Him PURE

New LAW AGAINST THE SALE OF COFFEE

Of course, despite the fears it stirred in its nascence,
coffee became popular around the world.

But it is still questioned from time to time.

In 1820, *caffe-ine* was discovered from the seed of a coffee cherry.

Caffeine is the plant's bitter alkaloid. When extracted from the seed, it crystallizes into silky threads to form a fleecy, toxic powder. It can cause anxiety, dependency, and, with overdose, even death.

It is the most popular stimulant on earth.

In 1910, a company from Atlanta, Georgia, was sued for its use of caffeine, which had become regarded as a habit-forming drug.

Consider the testimony, taken during the trial, of Dr. Oliver Osborne:

Q.   Now, Doctor, do you think that coffee and tea should be barred by law or otherwise?

A.   Well, I think it would be very quickly barred if young people could run constantly to a drugstore counter and get coffee and tea—

Q.   [*Interrupting*] Do you know whether or not they are doing it, Doctor?

A.   They soon get a physician if they do.

Q. Now, as a matter of fact, assuming that they do not do that, do you think coffee or tea or like products should be barred by law or otherwise?

A. You can't bar a beverage that is considered simple, but I will re-state that if it was known that our schoolchildren, or our young girls and boys, in shops or in stores were running in a store, or somewhere, and getting cups of coffee and cups of tea several times a day, it would soon be stopped, and physicians would get on to it, we would talk to the families, and it would soon become public in the paper, and such methods as seemed best would be taken to stop it.

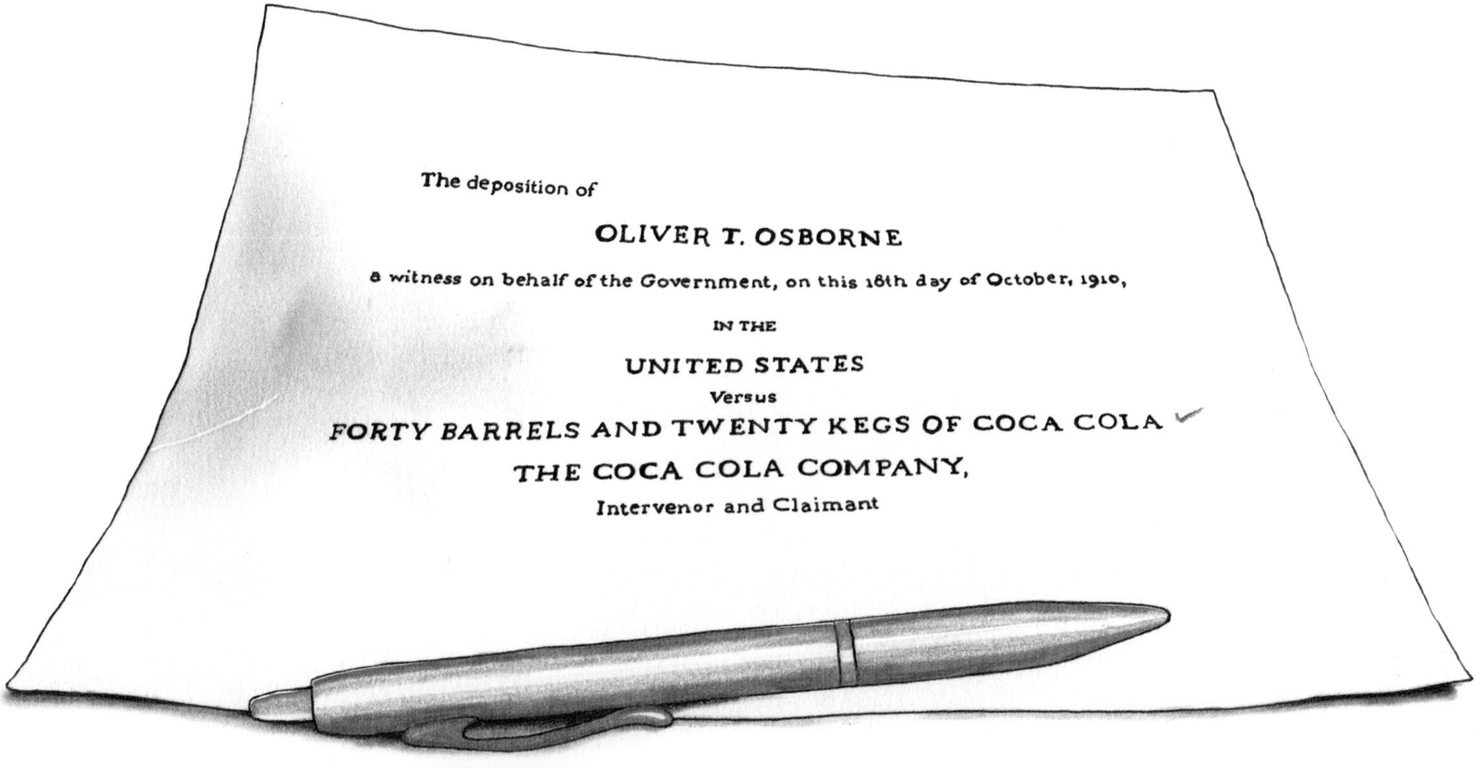

The deposition of

OLIVER T. OSBORNE

a witness on behalf of the Government, on this 18th day of October, 1910,

IN THE

UNITED STATES

Versus

FORTY BARRELS AND TWENTY KEGS OF COCA COLA

THE COCA COLA COMPANY,

Intervenor and Claimant

THE ATLANTA CONSTITUTION.

VOL. XVIII.   ATLANTA, GA., THURSDAY MORNING. JULY 1 1886   PRICE FIVE CENTS

CLOSED UP.

The Scenes on the Streets During the Last Days.

The Atlanta Saloons a Thing of the Past.

DRY ATLANTA—HOW SHE LOOKS

The Day Dawns and Goes Out Rainy and Wet.

AND WITH IT WHISKY GOES TOO.

But No One Gets Hurt and all Go Home Happy.

Part Two · Cola and Coca

Caffeine has been found in dozens of plants and seeds.

In West Africa, *kola* nuts are a rich source of caffeine and have been chewed throughout history as a stimulant and strengthener. It is used today at work, in ceremony, and socially.

Kola can be brewed too, to make a drink called *cola*.

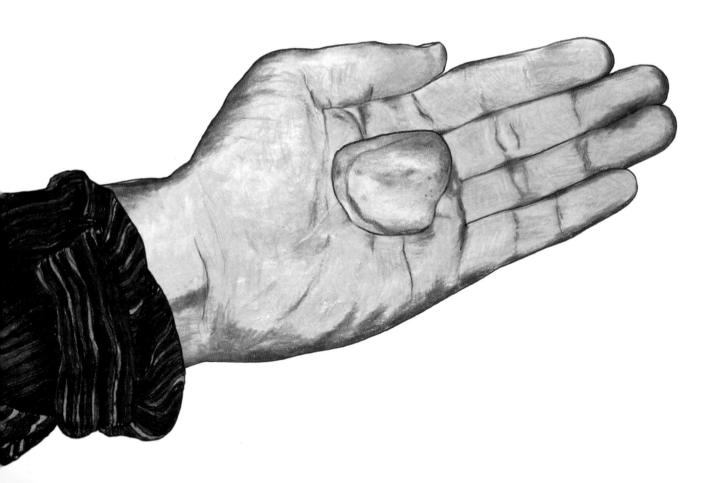

Cola is one of the most popular beverages on earth.

The most popular cola, *Coca-Cola*, was invented by Dr. John Pemberton, a pharmacist who mixed the kick of kola caffeine with a kick of *coca*.

Coca grows in the Andean mountains of South America.

Like the seeds of coffee and kola plants, coca leaves bestow a power of endurance when chewed. Coca has been used by people for thousands of years.

In August 1499, Amerigo Vespucci, sailing northwest along the coast of Venezuela, encountered an island of men with the leaf tucked in their cheeks.

For centuries thereafter, Europeans heard astonishing tales of the plant fueling marathons across mountains without food or rest.

Endow'd with Leaves of wondrous Nourishment,
Whose Juice suck'd in, and to the Stomach ta'n
Long Hunger and long Labour can sustain
                    —Abraham Cowley, 1689

On April 30, 1857, Dr. Karl Scherzer left Austria aboard the frigate *Novara,* as member of a scientific corps that included a botanist, a zoologist, an artist, and a flower gardener. Scherzer carried the request of a German pharmacologist to procure sixty pounds of coca for study. After two years Scherzer left the *Novara* to travel by foot into Peru. He returned to Europe in 1859 with the leaves. The coca was given to a young doctoral student, Albert Niemann, who discovered an alkaloid as the plant's active principle. Like *caffe-ine*, it was named after its parent: *coca-ine*—transparent crystals that congealed to a flaky white powder.

At first, experiments with cocaine were confined to medical practice.

In 1884, Sigmund Freud began to use it as a treatment for depression. He was enthralled by the "magical substance" and enthusiastically introduced it to colleagues and friends, including an oculist named Carl Koller. By then, cocaine's numbing effect had been observed on the tongue. Koller tested cocaine as a regional anesthetic; first on the eyes of animals and then his own. His discovery was a medical revolution.

Previously, surgeries were performed with general anesthesia or none at all. Ether and chloroform allowed severe operations without pain, although with significant risks from inducing unconsciousness. As the first true local anesthetic, cocaine opened the practice of surgery to previously impossible procedures.

Cocaine's popularity spread to other branches of therapy, and its use quickly grew beyond anesthesia and melancholia.

Cocaine eased toothaches and labor pains. It was said to cure fatigue, nervousness, impotence, even addiction to the opium poppy's alkaloid *morphine*. "Coke" could be purchased in asthma medicines, snuffs, and tonics like Coca-Cola—"The Brain Workers' Panacea," touted to relieve mental and physical exhaustion, was first sold in 1886.

Cases of compulsive use gained attention, and in 1889 the New York Academy of Medicine hosted a forum on the potential for cocaine abuse. Dr. Koller himself was invited. He praised therapeutic properties of the drug but also asked the assembly: "One did not give chloroform and ether to patients to be used by them indiscriminately, and why make cocaine an exception?"

Increased availability across race and class furthered problems associated with the habit, and a backlash emerged fueled by racial fears: cocaine made Negroes insane and murderous; Jewish doctors were identified as its peddlers.

Within thirty years, a medical miracle was transformed into a crime epidemic. Distinction between the coca plant and its alkaloid was lost in the rising fervor.

In 1914, the United States began prohibition of coca with the Harrison Narcotics Act.

Just eleven years earlier, The Coca-Cola Company began working with a German cocainemaker, Dr. Louis Schaefer, importing Peruvian coca leaf to his chemical plant in Maywood, New Jersey.

Schaefer Alkaloid Works supplied ingredients to Coca-Cola, including caffeine from coffee beans and tea dust, and a mixture of kola and a non-narcotic coca "flavoring extract." This secret formula was dubbed "Merchandise No. 5."

Over one hundred years later, this curiosity still stands.

Subsequently called Maywood Chemical Works, the site was acquired by the Stepan Chemical Company in 1959.

During the past century, coca became illegal in most countries around the world, sparking one of the longest, most expensive, and violent wars in history.

And thousands of tons of coca leaf were shipped to this secure, discreet facility.

Much credit can go to Harry Anslinger and Ralph Hayes.

MAYWOOD CHEMICAL WORKS

MAYWOOD, N.J.

September 26, 1930.

Hon. H. J. Anslinger,
Bureau of Narcotics,
Washington, D. C.

My dear Sir:-

I have just learned with great pleasure
and satisfaction that the President has appointed
you Commissioner of Narcotics.

The President has certainly made an
excellent choice and I beg you to accept my
heartiest congratulations.

Sincerely yours

Eugene Schaefer.
PRESIDENT

ES:AW.

In 1930, Harry J. Anslinger became commissioner of the US Federal Bureau of Narcotics. He led the ban against coca, while simultaneously helping secure The Coca-Cola Company's special access to it, through the administrations of seven presidents, until his retirement from government in 1970.

Ralph Hayes, former aide to the US Secretary of War, was a Washington businessman known for preserving important associations with powerful people. Hayes was hired by Coca-Cola in 1932 and began a friendship with Anslinger that grew over the next three decades.

TREASURY DEPARTMENT
BUREAU OF NARCOTICS
WASHINGTON

OFFICE OF
COMMISSIONER OF NARCOTICS

April 7, 1937.

Memorandum for the Secretary:

This case concerns two petitions submitted on behalf of The Coca Cola Company for a ruling permitting the exportation of "Merchandise No. 5", the basis for the drink Coca Cola, and to reverse a ruling heretofore made prohibiting such exportation. The General Counsel has held that the Narcotic Drugs Import and Export Act does not apply to Merchandise No. 5, and it follows that there is no foundation for the existing prohibition, and that prohibition is now revoked.

H. J. Anslinger,
Commissioner.

Enclosure

The Coca-Cola Company

WILMINGTON, DEL.

RALPH HAYES
VICE PRESIDENT

April 20, 1937

Honorable Harry J. Anslinger
Bureau of Narcotics
Tower Building
Washington, D. C.

Dear Mr. Commissioner:

When talking with you on Saturday I didn't want to impose further on your time by referring to the Department's recent ruling on the exportability of "Merchandise No. 5" but I do want you to know how deeply we appreciate the cooperativeness that has marked your personal attitude in this matter.

With this question now behind us, let me assure you again that our purpose, as always, will be to support every project looking to the enhancement of the prestige of the Bureau that has been so well developed under your distinguished leadership. Particularly, I am bearing in mind the items we discussed on Saturday and I shall get further word to you before you leave the country next week.

With warm regards, I am,

Sincerely yours,

Ralph Hayes

Commissioner Anslinger was a notorious antidrug zealot, best known for his relentless crusade against the marijuana plant. But he was an integral supporter to the coca business of Coca-Cola and Maywood, forwarding them relevant State Department reports, prying media inquires, and intelligence on South American coca farmers along with maps of their cocaine factories. As the law against coca evolved, Anslinger was consulted by and cooperated with Hayes and Maywood executives on legislative phraseology.

Coca-Cola's privilege to coca leaf was codified alongside the very laws that would prohibit its traditional users from growing it.

MAYWOOD CHEMICAL WORKS

MAYWOOD, N.J.

1944 JAN 19 AM 9 22

BUREAU OF NARCOTICS
MAILS AND FILES

January 17, 1944

Hon. H. J. Anslinger, Commissioner
Bureau of Narcotics
Treasury Department
Washington, D. C.

Dear Mr. Anslinger:

It is gratifying to know that even during the turmoil and dislocations of war, there has been no relaxation in the fight this country is making to rid the world of the illegitimate use of narcotics. I am particularly glad to note that credit for this is publicly and so properly attributed to your untiring efforts towards this end.

With all good wishes for your continued success, I am

Sincerely,
MAYWOOD CHEMICAL WORKS

M. J. Hartung
President

MJH:ra

---

y 12, 1948

H. J. Anslinger, Commissioner of Narcotics
Treasury Department
Bureau of Narcotics
Washington 25, D. C.

Dear Mr. Anslinger:

We quoted Mr. Hutchings a price of $5.50 per ounc for cocaine based on a purity of 90%, f.a.s. New York. Thi is below the material cost to us at Maywood, as coca leaf osts us 57¢ per pound delivered Maywood and contains appro tely 1% cocaine alkaloids.

In connection with this matter we will have furth ation for you when we have lunch together in Washing ay, the 16th Instant.

Sincerely,

MAYWOOD CHEMICAL WORK

MAYWOOD CHEMICAL WORKS

ESTABLISHED 1895

MAYWOOD, N.J.

M. J. HARTUNG
VICE PRESIDENT AND SECRETARY

Monday, April 8, 1940.

VISIT TO SIMBAL

Dr. Schaefer and I flew from Lima to Trujillo, arriving shortly after 1:00 P.M. Sr. Alfredo Pinillos and his brother, Victor, met us at the airport. We motored into town and picked up

When the Coca reaches the warehouse in Trujillo, Pinillos examines each sack and rejects any coca which is not of prime quality. Unless it is thoroughly dry, he further dries it in his warehouse and then bales it for shipment to Maywood.

The coca is shipped from Trujillo to Salaverry by rail, and then lightered to the steamer.

Pinillos offered to drive us to Sacamaca, whence we also receive coca. It is 130 kilometers from Trujillo at an altitude (2800 to 3000 feet).

December 2, 194

orable H. J. Anslinger, Commissioner
reau of Narcotics
easury Department
shington, D. C.

ear Mr. Anslinger:

Yesterday I received two copies howing the coca growing areas and the loc ocaine factories in Peru. Because of our Peru these maps are especially interesting ppreciate your having sent them.

With all good wishes.

Sincerely,

MAYWOOD CHEMICAL W

M. J. Hartung
President

The Coca-Cola Company
WILMINGTON 99 DELAWARE

June 4, 1952.

Hon. Harry J. Anslinger
Shoreham Hotel
Washington 25, D. C.

Dear Mr. Commissioner:

It is always gratifying to me to read that "the system of import certificates . . . for the control of imports . . . of . . . coca leaves . . . has operated successfully . . . " and I imagine you find a degree of satisfaction in the revenue of $60,579.15 produced by coca leaf last year.

Your annual report is, as usual, an impressive and encouraging document.

Very truly yours,

Ralph Hayes

Apr. 13, 1951.

Hon. Walter F. George
Senate Office Building
Washington, D. C.

Dear Senator George:

Commissioner Harry J. Anslinger, in the twenty-one years since he was appointed by President Hoover, has, it seems to me, built up a truly remarkable organization and I would imagine that the Congress might be disposed to analyze any alternative closely before merging or transferring or otherwise altering one of the governmental agencies that is presently operating with outstanding efficiency.

The Congress might well find that, high as is the prestige of the Federal Bureau of Investigation and persuasive as is the generality of recommendations by the Hoover Commission, the present location and the existing standards of the Bureau of Narcotics are so satisfactory and so clearly in furtherance of the public interest as to place a heavy burden of proof on the proponents of any legislation contemplating the transfer, merger or alteration of this Bureau.

Very truly yours,

RALPH HAYES

UNITED STATES TREASURY DEPARTMENT
FLAVORING EXTRACT CERTIFIED NON NARCOTIC

Please Address Reply
c/o The Coca-Cola Co.
515 Madison Ave., NYC 22

July 5, 1956.

rry J. Anslinger
m Hotel
ton 25, D. C.

rry:

Though scarcely surprising, it is as always
ing to read in the report of the Bureau of Narcotics
5 that "The system . . . in force for the control of
. . . of . . . coca leaves . . . has operated satisfactoril
."

and.
ion.

Erythroxylonically yours,

RALPH HAYES

ROOM 1223
250 PARK AVENUE
NEW YORK 17, N.Y.

July 17, 1952

Commissioner Harry J. Anslinger
1300 E St. NW
Washington 25, D. C.

Dear Harry:

Some time back, you mentioned your willingness to commend me to your departmental associates in a way that might expedite in some degree my baggage examinations on returning from foreign trips.

elu iling myself of this thoughtful
ki
t f
e
e

ROOM 1223
250 PARK AVENUE
NEW YORK 17, N.Y.

Dear Harry:
You may wish to pass along this enclosure to the Library. It comes from the "Community Relief Fund" which you know about but that need not be mentioned in transmitting it unless you prefer to do so.
Sincerely yours
Ralph

ROOM 1223
250 PARK AVENUE
NEW YORK 17, N.Y.

November 9, 1954

Hon. Harry J. Anslinger
Shoreham Hotel
Washington 25, D.C.

Dear Harry:

It was good of you to telephone this morning and, particularly, to offer that "wrecking crew" of yours. I know the punch it packs! Don't demobilize it but hold it in abeyance: I'll call out if need arises.

Meanwhile, you and I have some pending homework that we should get at without too much delay. I'm a few hundred yards from your UN shop and if other errands call you there before I'm sprung from here, we ought to continue the talk we began at our last luncheon.

Sincerely yours,

Ralph

RH J

In turn, Ralph Hayes used his political influence, charm, and tactful contributions to support Anslinger's long tenure in Washington, DC.

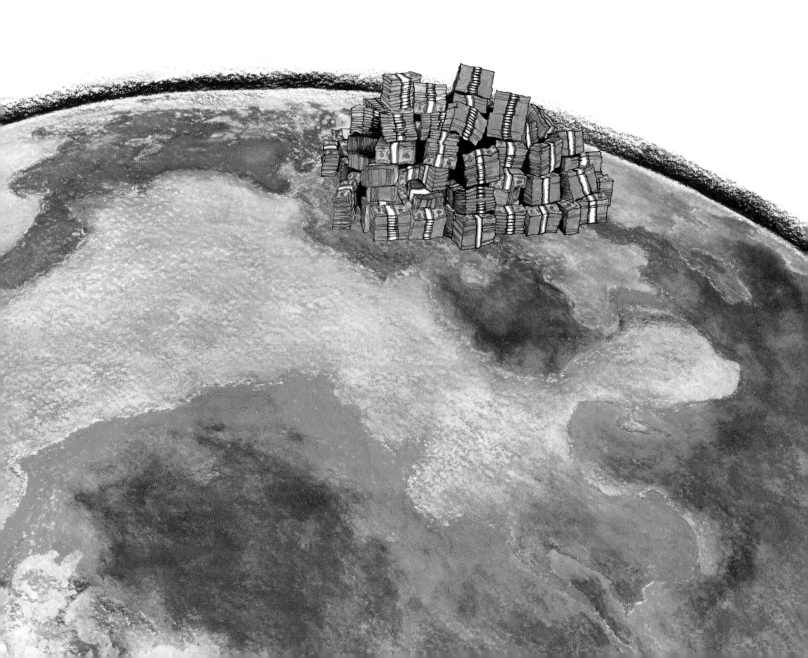

MAYWOOD CHEMICAL WORKS

M. J. HARTUNG
PRESIDENT

MAYWOOD, N. J.

September 17, 1951

Hon. H. J. Anslinger, Commissioner
Bureau of Narcotics
U. S. Treasury Department
Washington 25, D. C.

Dear Mr. Anslinger:

The Commission on Narcotic Drugs of the United Nations has for several years been endeavoring to effect a unification of the many conventions on narcotic drugs which were adopted by the League of Nations at various times since 1912. The advantages of such a unification are apparent.

The Bulletin on Narcotics, Vol. II, No.

SINGLE CONVENTION

RALPH HAYES
Hotel DuPont
Wilmington 99, Del.

May 5, 1955

Commissioner Harry J. Anslinger
Hotel Shoreham
Washington, D. C.

Dear Harry:

The U. N. debate regarding the categories of the legitimate uses of coca leaves to be inserted in the Single Convention took me by surprise. After your thoughtfulness in permitting me to read Dr. Lande's memorandum on "The Use of Coca Leaves for Flavouring Purposes Under the Single Convention", I had supposed that the matter was in an agreed and favorable status.

It was most fortunate that you intervened in the Commission's proceedings as deftly and decisively as you did and that your position was sustained - with the support, I infer, of our friends from Canada, the United Kingdom and Peru. It need scarcely be said that your action is most warmly gratifying.

With deepest appreciation, believe me,

Sincerely yours,

Ralph

RH J

MAYWOOD CHEMICAL WORKS
ESTABLISHED 1895
MAYWOOD, N. J.

April 30th, 1959.

Honorable H.J.Anslinger,
Treasury Department,
Bureau of Narcotics,
Washington, 25, D.C.

Dear Mr. Anslinger:

I am delighted to have your letter of the 29th and fervently wish success to your plans.

The smooth and economical operation of our process demands an ample and constant supply of Coca and I am happy to note that you realize the importance of liberal stocks of Coca for medicinal needs and for our special purpose.

RALPH HAYES

March 16, 1960

Hon. Harry J. Anslinger
Hotel Shoreham
Washington, D. C.

Dear Harry:

It is understandable that the State Department should be earnestly desirous of your leading this country's delegation in person at the international narcotic conference next January. I can imagine that the Single Convention may rank as the most significant development in the history of world narcotic control and your presence and prestige will certainly constitute a formidable factor in the attainment of this global agreement that has been so long in negotiation.

Sincerely yours,

Ralph

Their mutual interests culminated during the drafting of the 1961 United Nations Single Convention on Narcotic Drugs.

By then, nine separate legal agreements between nations had created an overly complex system of drug laws. Following thirteen years of negotiation, the Single Convention was adopted to simplify and supersede all previous protocols. Today it is one of three treaties, along with the 1971 Convention on Psychotropic Substances and the 1988 Convention Against Illicit Traffic in Narcotic Drugs and Psychotropic Substances, that define the international drug control system.

Representing the United States, Harry Anslinger steered to outlaw the coca plant. The Single Convention, as adopted, orders people worldwide to stop chewing coca leaves, whether for health or culture, and mandates the uprooting and destruction of all wild bushes.

And it contains the provision that allows Coca-Cola to use coca.

After ratification of the Single Convention, Anslinger resigned from the Bureau of Narcotics and became US representative to the United Nations Narcotics Commission.

Although The Coca-Cola Company's access to coca was now legally secure, political instability in South America could pose a threat to its perpetual procurement. In 1962, Ralph Hayes asked Anslinger's successor, Henry L. Giordano, to permit Coca-Cola to grow coca in the United States. The company was interested in expanding its agronomic knowledge, Hayes wrote, especially of variance in cocaine content and flavor of the leaves.

The bureau's new commissioner guided Coca-Cola through legalities of the project. After initial inquires into the US Virgin Islands, fertile grounds of the University of Hawaii were chosen to host the experiment.

University President Thomas Hamilton initially demurred at the request to hide Coca-Cola's name from the project. "Certainly we shall not volunteer such information," he wrote to Coca-Cola's new vice president, Benjamin Oehlert Jr. "On the other hand, should questions be raised I shall have to answer them. Being a public university we really can have no secrets!"

Oehlert wrote to Giordano, asking if he "might feel it appropriate to intervene personally . . . expressing views of the Bureau first that the research contemplated would be desirable from your viewpoint, and second that the work should be regarded as classified and not subject to publication." Hamilton revised his position. "I think Commissioner Giordano's letter puts quite a different face on the matter," he wrote back to Oehlert.

Oehlert concluded: "The fact that The Coca-Cola Company was involved in putting the parties to the agreement together should, we feel, be of no consequence to anyone other than the parties themselves and the Bureau of Narcotics."

April 18, 1963

Mr. Ralph Hayes
Hotel duPont
Wilmington 99, Delaware

Dear Ralph:

This is in reply to your letter of April 5, 1963, wherein you indicate a desire to grow coca leaves for research purposes in the Hawaiian Islands.

You may be assured that we will do what we can to let the appropriate Hawaiian authorities know that your proposed project has the Bureau's approval. Since Hawaii is a State the situation is somewhat different than when you proposed to grow the coca leaves in the Virgin Islands. I would suggest that you may want to communicate with Dr. Leo Bernstein, Director of Health, Department of Health, Honolulu, Hawaii, or with Mr. George H. Akau, Chief of the Food and Drug Branch of the Department of Health, regarding any required permits or licenses which you might need.

Sincerely yours,

Henry L. Giordano
Commissioner of Narcotics

EXECUTIVE CHAMBERS
HONOLULU

JOHN A. BURNS
GOVERNOR

February 18, 1964

Dear Mr. Oehlert:

I was certain of President Hamilton's understanding in regard to the publicity on the Coca project.

As I have already assured you, I believe difficulties can be ironed out as we go along.

Warmest personal regards. May the Almighty be with you and yours always.

Sincerely,

John A. Burns

Mr. Benjamin H. Oehlert, Jr.
Vice President
The Coca-Cola Company
P. O. Box 2711
Orlando, Florida

cc: President Thomas H. Hamilton

INTERNAL REVENUE SERVICE
UNITED STATES OFFICIAL ORDER
FORM - OPIUM, COCA LEAVES,
OPIATES, ETC.

FORM 2513 (REV. 9-59)

PURCHASER MUST BE PROPERLY REG-
ISTERED FOR FISCAL YEAR BEFORE
USING THIS FORM. SUPPLIER MUST BE
PROPERLY REGISTERED FOR FISCAL
YEAR BEFORE HE MAY FILL IT.

THIS IS AN ORDER TO SUPPLY
THE DRUGS SPECIFIED BELOW

5TH N J CLASS 1 & 5 REG 4181
MAYWOOD CHEMICAL WORKS
DIVISION OF STEPAN CHEMICAL CO
100 W HUNTER AVE
MAYWOOD N J

NO. 4994473

TO University of Hawaii, College of Tropical Agriculture,
Hawaii Agricultural Experiment Station

NUMBER, STREET, CITY, STATE   Kauai.Branch Station,
Kapaa, Kauai, Hawaii

DATE 11/11/64
To be filled in by consignor

TO BE FILLED IN BY PURCHASER

ITEM	CATALOGUE NUMBER IF ANY	NUMBER OF PACKAGES	SIZE OF PACKAGE NO. OF LBS., OZ., GRAINS, PILLS, TAB., ETC. IN EACH PKG.	NAME OF ARTICLE NAME OF NARCOTIC DRUG INVOLVED MUST BE STATED	NO. OF PKGS. FUR-NISHED	DATE FILLED
1		1	up to 3#	Coca Leaf	1	11/16/64
2						
3						

NAME OF PERSON OR FIRM IF NOT AN INDIVIDUAL

Donald H. Francis

SIGNATURE OF PURCHASER, OR HIS ATTORNEY, OR AGENT
Donald H.Francis, V.Pres.&Gen'l Mngr.
Stepan Chemical Co. Maywood Division

"Cultural Studies in Coca" (code name: Ala Kea) began in 1964 at the Hawaii Agricultural Experiment Station on the island of Kauai.

Coca was found to grow in the Andean-like climate but was notably susceptible to an unknown disease. Thousands of additional seeds were imported from Peru, but seedlings continued to succumb to wilting and root rot.

Plant deaths increased throughout the 1970s, and the blight spread over ten acres of research plots. In 1982, Hurricane Iwa tore across Kauai and caused significant damage to the island. Ala Kea was terminated in 1984. According to researchers of the project, the remaining files deemed sensitive were destroyed.

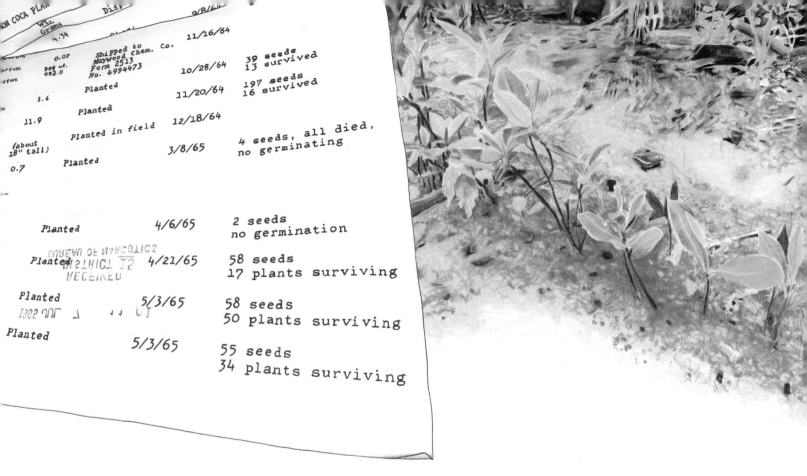

Planted   4/6/65   2 seeds
     no germination

Planted   4/21/65   58 seeds
     17 plants surviving

Planted   5/3/65   58 seeds
     50 plants surviving

Planted   5/3/65   55 seeds
     34 plants surviving

Interest in the disease prompted the US Department of Agriculture to take over the site with its research arm, the Agricultural Research Service. In November 1987, 1300 coca plants grown in Beltsville, Maryland, were transplanted to Kauai. The next year, a mycoherbicide (fungal pathogen), *Fusarium oxysporum,* was identified as the coca-killer.

In the 1990s, the White House and the State Department began to debate whether it was possible to use the mycoherbicide without violating international laws against biological weapons.

In April 2000, the United Nations Drug Control Program released a proposal for experimental field trials in Colombia. Under pressure from the United States, Colombian officials agreed to study *Fusarium oxysporum* for use in the Amazon. In late 2006, the White House authorized scientists from the National Research Council to examine the feasibility of developing fungi to eradicate illicit coca.

"The Board wishes to point out that, within 25 years following the entry into force of the 1961 Convention, coca leaf chewing should have been abolished in those countries where it was taking place. As the 1961 Convention came into force in 1964, coca leaf chewing should have come to an end in 1989. In addition, coca leaf is used in Bolivia and Peru for the manufacture and distribution of coca tea. Such use is also not in line with the provisions of the 1961 Convention . . . The Board reminds all Governments that importation of coca leaf for purposes other than medical and scientific purposes or the preparation of a flavouring agent is contrary to the provisions of the 1961 Convention."

—The International Narcotics Control Board of the United Nations, 2007

That same year . . .

World coffee production was around 7 million tonnes of beans.

Cocaine production was around one thousand tonnes.

The Coca-Cola Company sold almost 135 million tonnes of beverages.

Stepan Chemical Company imported forty-five tonnes of coca.

In the US, law enforcement made more arrests for illegal drugs than any other crime, incarcerating forty-three thousand tonnes of human flesh.

With a federal drug control budget of over 13 billion dollars, it made us a costly meat . . . almost $140 a pound.

But that's another story.

The cat won't stop catching mice,
and young ladies will hold to their coffee.
Mother loves her coffee,
Grandmother drinks it, too.
Who, in the end, would scold the daughters?
—*The Chorus*

Appendix and Selected Bibliography

Schlendrian, Liesgen, and the Chorus
Quotations are from *Kaffee Kantate: Schweigt stille, plaudert nicht,* by Johann Sebastian Bach and Christian Friedrich Henrici (1734).
   BWV 211. (*Coffee Cantata: Be Silent, Don't Chatter,* Trans. Sareeta Amrute.)

From Coffee to Caffeine
Watts, Henry. *A Dictionary of Chemistry Vol. I.* London: Longmans, Green, & Co., 1863.
Robinson, Edward. *The Early English Coffee House.* 1893. New Zealand: Dolphin Press, Christchurch, 1972.
Ukers, William H. *All About Coffee.* 2nd ed. New York: The Tea & Coffee Trade Journal Company, 1935.
Birnbaum, E. "Vice Triumphant: The Spread of Coffee and Tobacco in Turkey." *Durham University Journal,* December 1956: 21–27.
Hattox, Ralph S. *Coffee and Coffeehouses: Origins of a Social Beverage in Medieval Near East.* Seattle: Univ. of Washington Press, 1985.
Spiller, Gene A., ed. *Caffeine.* Los Altos, CA: Health Research and Studies Center and Sphera Foundation, 1998.
Pendergrast, Mark. *Uncommon Grounds: The History of Coffee and How It Transformed Our World.* New York: Basic Books, 1999.
Wild, Antony. *Coffee: A Dark History.* New York: W.W. Norton & Company, 2004.

On Kola
Menninger, Edwin. *Edible Nuts of the World.* Stuart, FL: Horticultural Books, 1977.
Rosengarten, Frederic Jr. *The Book of Edible Nuts.* Walker and Company, 1984.
Abaka, Edmund. *Kola Is God's Gift.* Ohio University Press, 2005.

On the Origin of Coca-Cola
"Coca-Cola Advertisement." *Atlanta Journal.* May 29, 1886; June 16, 1886; January 7, 1887; June 16, 1887.
"Coca-Cola Advertisement." *Scientific American.* Vol. XCV No.1. July 7, 1906: 15.
Kahn, E.J., Jr. *The Big Drink: The Story of Coca-Cola.* New York: Random House, 1960.
Munsey, Cecil. *The Illustrated Guide to the Collectibles of Coca-Cola.* New York: Hawthorn Books, 1972.
Pendergrast, Mark. *For God, Country & Coca-Cola.* New York: Basic Books, 2000.

On Coca
The First Four Voyages of Amerigo Vespucci: Translated From the Rare Original Edition (Florence, 1505–6). London: Bernard Quaritch, 1885.
The Third Part of the Works of M'Abraham Cowley, Being His Six Books of Plants. London: Printed for Charles Harper, 1689.
Mariani, Vin. *Coca Erythroxylon: Its Uses in the Treatment of Disease.* Paris: Mariani & Company, 1884.
Mortimer, W. Golden. *History of Coca: "The Divine Plant" of the Incas.* 1901. California: AND/OR Press, 1974.
Weil, Andrew. "The New Politics of Coca." *New Yorker.* May 15, 1995: 70–80.

From Coca to Cocaine
Scherzer, Karl. *Voyage of the Novara: Narrative of the Circumnavigation of the Globe.* Vol. 3. London: Saunders, Otley, & Co., 1863.
Knapp, Herman. *Cocaine and Its Use in Ophthalmic and General Surgery.* New York: G.P. Putnam's Sons, 1885.
"The Indiscriminate Use of Cocaine." *New York Medical Journal.* December 28, 1889: 719–20.
"The Growing Menace of the Use of Cocaine." *New York Times.* August 2, 1908: 1.
Congressional Record 50, pt. 3: 2191–2211. 63rd United States Congress First Session. June 26, 1913.
Jones, Ernest. *The Life and Work of Sigmund Freud.* New York: Basic Books, 1961.
Taylor, Arnold. *American Diplomacy and the Narcotics Traffic, 1900–1939.* Durham, NC: Duke University Press, 1969.
Kennedy, Joseph. *Coca Exotica: The Illustrated Story of Cocaine.* New Jersey: Associated University Presses, 1985.
Musto, David. *The American Disease: Origins of Narcotic Control.* Oxford University Press, 1999.
Spillane, Joseph. *Cocaine: From Medical Marvel to Modern Menace in the United States, 1884–1920.* John Hopkins University Press, 2000.
Gootenberg, Paul. *Andean Cocaine: The Making of a Global Drug.* Chapel Hill, NC: University of North Carolina Press, 2008.

Notes on the Illustrations Thus Far . . .
The drawing of *Eazy-E* is based on a photograph by Ernie Paniccioli. **Kubrick Demonstrates How to Shoot the Coke Machine** is of a photo from *The Stanley Kubrick Archives* (Taschen), edited by Alison Castle, used with permission of the Stanley Kubrick Estate. *Coca Kola Girl* is based on a photo by Daniela Crespo. *Three Surgeons* is based on a photo from the Bellevue Hospital Archives, New York City. *Newsboy* is based on a photo by Lewis Wickes Hine/Library of Congress; the *Newspaper* he holds is "Negro Cocaine 'Fiends' are a New Southern Menace: Murder and Insanity Increasing Among Lower Class Blacks Because They Have Taken to 'Sniffing' Since Deprived of Whisky by Prohibition" by Williams, Edward H. *New York Times.* Feb. 8, 1914: SM12.

About the Correspondence

Some letters have been edited for length, but great effort was made to ensure the writers' intentions and meanings have not been interfered with, distorted, or misrepresented. The letters are drawn in pencil, pen, and color pencil, based on the author's photographs of original documents from:

Subject files of the Bureau of Narcotics and Dangerous Drugs. Record Group 170: Boxes 20, 23, 63, 64, 141, 170. US National Archives, MD.

H.J. Anslinger Papers, 1835–1970. Accession 1959-0006H, Historical Collections and Labor Archives, Special Collections Library, University Libraries, Pennsylvania State University, University Park, PA.

Maywood, Anslinger, and Hayes

Depositions of Dr. Louis Schaefer and Hugo DuBois taken Oct. 19, 1910. *United States v. Forty Barrels and Twenty Kegs of Coca Cola.* 191 F. 431 (E.D. Tenn. 1911), rev'd, 241 US 265 (1916).

"Other Sales, Mergers." *New York Times.* May 12, 1959: 49.

McWilliams, John C. "Unsung Partner Against Crime: Harry J. Anslinger and the Federal Bureau of Narcotics, 1930–1962." *The Pennsylvania Magazine of History and Biography.* Vol. 113, No. 2. April 1989: 207–236.

Lande, Adolf. *The Single Convention on Narcotic Drugs.* International Organization, Vol. 16, No. 4. Cambridge University Press, 1962.

"Ralph Hayes, Noted Fund-Raiser; Led New York Community Trust." *New York Times.* June 22, 1977: 28.

May, Clifford D. "How Coca-Cola Obtains Its Coca." *New York Times.* July 1, 1988: D1.

Miller, Michael W. "Quality Stuff: Firm Is Peddling Cocaine, and Deals Are Legit—Stepan Imports Coca Leaves for Medicinal Purposes and a Very Special Client." *Wall Street Journal.* October 27, 1994: A1.

Chauvin, Lucien O. "Peruvian Firm Exports Coca Leaves." *Miami Herald.* July 4, 2003.

Gootenberg, Paul. "Secret Ingredients: The Politics of Coca in US–Peruvian Relations, 1915–65." *Journal of Latin American Studies* 36. Cambridge University Press, 2004: 233–265.

Single Convention on Narcotic Drugs 1961, as amended by the 1972 Protocol Amending the Single Convention on Narcotic Drugs.

esp. Articles 26, 27, 49. United Nations: New York.

Hawaii

Darlington, Lee. "History of Erythroxylum and Notes on Diseases and Pests at Kauai Field Site." *Proceedings of the 1st International Workshop on Fusarium Biocontrol.* Beltsville, MD. October 28–31, 1996: 43.

"Characterization of a Vascular Wilt of Erythroxylum coca . . ." Sands, D.C.; Ford, E.J.; Miller, R.V.; Sally, B.K.; McCarthy, M.K.; Anderson, T.W.; Weaver, M.B.; Morgan, C.T.; Pilgeram, A.L.; and Darlington, L.C. *Plant Disease*, Vol. 81 No. 5, 1997: 501–504.

Golden, Tim. "Fungus Considered As a Tool to Kill Coca in Colombia." *New York Times.* July 6, 2000.

Public Law 109–469—Dec. 29, 2006 Office of National Drug Control Policy Reauthorization Act of 2006. [H.R. 6344]

E-mail exchange with Jim Cartwright (University Archivist, University of Hawaii) and Dr. Jeri Ooka (Mycologist, UH). April 2009.

Phone interview with Dr. Jeri Ooka (Mycologist, Kauai Agricultural Research Center, University of Hawaii). November 17, 2010.

Feasibility of Using Mycoherbicides for Controlling Illicit Drug Crops. National Research Council. The National Academies Press, DC, 2011.

2007

Report of the International Narcotics Control Board for 2007. United Nations Publication ISBN: 978-92-1-148224-9. New York, 2008.

International Coffee Agreement September 2007 and *Coffee Market Report March 2008* International Coffee Organization.

United Nations World Drug Report 2009. United Nations Publication ISBN: 978-92-1-148240-9. New York, 2009.

Annual Report Form 10-K for the fiscal year ended December 31, 2007, The Coca-Cola Company. US Securities and Exchanges Commission. Washington, DC, 2008: 42-3. (12 fl. oz. of Coca-Cola weighs approx. 368.8 grams [Ohaus balance, 5/5/09]).

Memoria 2007 (Annual Report 2007). La Empresa Nacional de la Coca S.A., Peru, 2008: 21.

Sabol, William J.; West, Heather C. *Bureau of Justice Statistics, Prisoners in 2007.* US Department of Justice NCJ224280. Dec. 2008: 22.

National Drug Control Strategy FY2008. Office of National Drug Control Policy. The White House, February 2007.

Price per pound: Est. 500,000 US drug prisoners [Mauer, Marc; Ryan S. King. "A 25-Year Quagmire: The War on Drugs and Its Impact on American Society." The Sentencing Project. Washington, DC, September 2007]; the average person held in state and federal custody (by race, sex, age) was a black male of 25–29 years [Sabol and West: 19]; such a man's average weight was roughly 190 pounds ["Anthropometric Reference Data for Children and Adults: US Population, 1999–2002." Centers for Disease Control and Prevention, National Center for Health Statistics. AD No. 361, July 7, 2005: Table 30]; then the total weight of drug war prisoners was, very roughly, 95 million pounds.

Epilogue

Note by the secretary-general on the proposal of amendments by Bolivia to article 49, paragraphs 1 (c) and 2 (e), of the Single Convention on Narcotic Drugs, 1961, as amended by the Protocol amending the Single Convention on Narcotic Drugs, 1961 (E/2009/78). U.N. ECOSOC. May 15, 2009.

Press conference. Pablo Solon, Representative of Bolivia. June 24, 2011. *UN Webcast:* www.UNmultimedia.org/tv/webcast/ [accessed 2/21/12]

Memoria 2010 (Annual Report 2010). La Empresa Nacional de la Coca S.A., Peru, 2012: 26.

The author would like to acknowledge reportage of the Single Convention treaty by the Andean Information Network (www.ain-bolivia.org); and the Drug Law Reform Project of the Transnational Institute (www.tni.org) and the Washington Office on Latin America (www.wola.org).

Epilogue

In March 2009, Bolivian president Evo Morales Ayma stood before the United Nations with a formal request to correct the "historical error" of the 1961 Single Convention. He cited thousands of years of coca use for purposes social, spiritual, medicinal, and nutritional. Then he put a leaf of coca in his mouth, sparking applause from the assembly.

"Coca leaf chewing is one of the sociocultural practices and rituals of the Andean indigenous peoples. It is closely linked to our history and cultural identity. Today it is practised by millions of people in Bolivia, Peru, northern Argentina and Chile, Ecuador and Colombia . . . The objective of the Single Convention on Narcotic Drugs of 1961 is to control drug abuse, not to prohibit 'habits' or sociocultural practices that do not harm human health."

The president's proposed amendment to the treaty was denied by the United States.

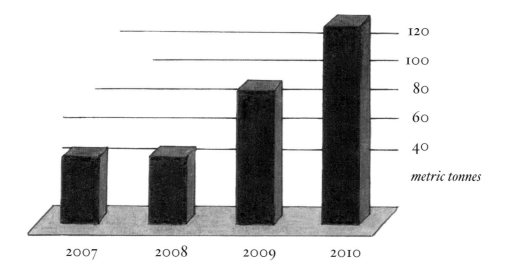

In 2010, Stepan Chemical Company coca imports tripled, since 2007, from 45 to 136 tonnes.

In 2011, Bolivia announced it would withdraw from the Single Convention and then rejoin again–an odd technicality that would allow the country to include a denouncement of coca prohibition amidst its obligation to the treaty. The denunciation took effect in January 2012.

Coca remains prohibited for ten million or so people who chew it.

"Some time a studious historian searching for the occasions and causes of the prohibition era in the United States will pen an interesting paragraph about the 'soft' drink called coca-cola . . ."

—*New York Times*, March 14, 1929

Author's Note

The transformation of cultural and legal taboos against plants fascinates me. The arc of discovery, experimentation, prohibition, and reconsideration of inebriants is not unique to apples, potatoes, or coffee, nor will it end with marijuana, tobacco, or coca.

For my research I visited Hawaiian coffee fields, a coca farm in the Chapare of Bolivia, and the Stepan Chemical plant in Maywood, NJ. I asked the Drug Enforcement Administration about Stepan's coca imports and manufacturing of cocaine. I spoke with representatives of The Coca-Cola Company—on the subject of coca, I was told more than once: "As much as I would like to answer this specific inquiry, I am not able to comment on matters relating to the formula, which is one of our most valuable assets."

I spoke with journalists, historians, activists, archivists, lawyers, botanists, a chemist, and a captain of the Maywood Police Department. Special thanks to Paul Gootenberg, whose research in an article for the *Journal of Latin American Studies* tipped me to files of the Federal Bureau of Narcotics in the US National Archives. I spent days there, combing through boxes and photographing declassified correspondence. I similarly documented the letters of Harry J. Anslinger from the collections of Pennsylvania State University. By combining hundreds of pages in chronological order, a conversation of politics and friendship emerged spanning decades.

A note on my illustration technique: all the images in this book were made with pencil, pen, and (mostly) color pencil. The drawings of letters are based on the original pages I photographed in 2009–2011. Some letters have been edited for length, but great effort was made to ensure the writers' intentions and meanings have not been interfered with, distorted, or misrepresented.

This book could not have been made without help from librarians, especially of the New York Public Libraries; the National Archives at College Park, Maryland; the Special Collections Library of Pennsylvania State University; the New York Academy of Medicine Library; the Drug Policy Alliance; the Horticultural Society of New York; and the Brooklyn Public Library.

For more information, please visit: **CoffeeCocaCola.com**

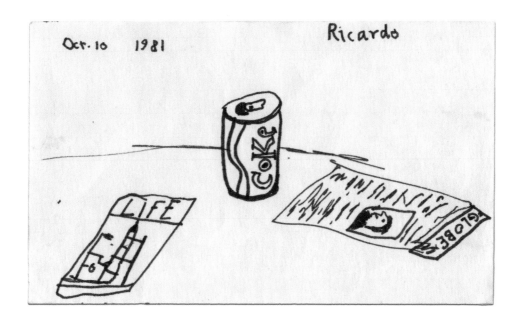

About the Author

Ricardo Cortés has written and illustrated books such as *It's Just a Plant: A Children's Story about Marijuana* and *I Don't Want to Blow You Up!* He is also the illustrator of the best-selling *Go the Fuck to Sleep*, along with the book's kid sister, *Seriously, Just Go to Sleep*.

He is working on a book about a shark.

RMCORTES.COM